wild rice dreams

vera wabegijig

BookLand press

Published by BookLand Press
15 Allstate Parkway, Suite 600, Markham, Ontario L3R 5B4
www.booklandpress.com

Printed and bound in Canada

Front cover image © Rolffimages | Dreamstime.com

Library and Archives Canada Cataloguing in Publication

Wabegijig, Vera, author
Wild rice dreams : Canadian Aboriginal voices / Vera Wabegijig.

Issued in print and electronic formats.
ISBN 978-1-926956-63-3 (pbk.).--ISBN 978-1-926956-64-0 (epub).--ISBN 978-1-926956-65-7 (pdf)

I. Title.

PS8645.A32W55 2013 C811'.6 C2013-903695-4
C2013-903696-2

Canada Council for the Arts | Conseil des arts du Canada

ONTARIO ARTS COUNCIL
CONSEIL DES ARTS DE L'ONTARIO
50 YEARS OF ONTARIO GOVERNMENT SUPPORT OF THE ARTS
50 ANS DE SOUTIEN DU GOUVERNEMENT DE L'ONTARIO AUX ARTS

We acknowledge the support of the Canada Council for the Arts, which last year invested $157 million to bring the arts to Canadians throughout the country. We acknowledge the support of the Ontario Arts Council (OAC), an agency of the Government of Ontario, which last year funded 1,681 individual artists and 1,125 organizations in 216 communities across Ontario for a total of $52.8 million. We acknowledge the financial support of the Ontario Media Development Corporation for our publishing activities.

dedicated to my daughters, storm and grace,
who helped me to become the mother
and woman i am

table of contents

part one
this native land

part two
look around us

part three
tending dreams and memories

part four
all in the family

part one

this native land

words of my ancestors

my ancestors passed on many words to me
words that make up stories
stories that breathe life into me
stories that remind me of who i am
and where i come from
where the blood flows through lifelines
where the spirits sit by fires
where stories and songs begin and don't end
they passed on knowledge
and the strength in knowledge
knowledge that digs into the earth taking root
these roots spread beyond any sense of time
ancestors root deep into my being
my blood - my memory
my blood memory
they passed on the sacredness of all life
they passed on songs that carry heartbeats
a beat ignites words
words grow knowledge
knowledge spreads seeds
seeds take root into the earth
earth creates a beat
beat carries a song
they passed on and breathed words
words resonate beats
beats rhythm songs
songs give life
life beats stories
stories breathe truth to me
to you, to creation, to ancestors

drum song

i wanna be a drum
made from deer skin
stretching, reaching for the edges
where sinew meets and braids crisscross
a hand holds in a firm grip
yielding to the songs you sing
yielding to a beat you carry deep within
and a breath you hold steady
as a song forms from dreams

i wanna be a drum
you carry in the bag nokimis made
from an old pair of wranglers
and a leftover ribbon shirt
stitched together in a seam of protection
you carry me close
protecting me from bad medicine
bad thoughts and bad memories

i wanna be a drum
you bring on the pow-wow trail
wrapped in a star blanket
you paint me with sacred ochre
and tie eagle feathers around me
you offer me saamaa
and pray for me
to become one with you

i wanna be a drum
at a round dance
with one hand you hold me close to your body
while the other hand circles round and round
as you murmur prayers to me
heating my surface
so that i will speak true with a strong voice
and my deer skin will breathe
deep resonating beats

the drum warrior

in one hand
the drum
                    - an instrument of love

in the other hand
a drum stick
                    - a symbol of what's to come

he taps along the drum's edge
heart beats
across tundra, wetlands, boreal and rainforest
his voice rises and echoes off concrete walls

tonight
he knows a new power

a drum, a stick, a song
stokes lingering embers
glowing on a cold winter's night

in indian country

where skins gather inside a community hall
escaping winter's frosty breath
as cars and trucks idle in parking lots
exhaust pipes puff out white clouds
with crispy edges
against a star-filled night

indians are all lined up on the bleachers
the heat gathers and goes past many layers
this gym is steaming
jackets, toques and rabbit-lined deer gloves
with floral designs
are folded on laps
heads beat in sync

on the floor
chorus raises
past the rafters
past the championship banners that hang
hockey, basketball and soccer reign supreme
hands pump up and down
boots clump-slide stepping
around gathered drums
in the middle of a restless winter's night

it is not fair

a mother walks her daughter
along the addict-infested sidewalks
to the inner-city school
that waits with open doors
each morning yard monitors pick up needles
making it safe for games

cops who catch the robbers
cowboys who kill the indians

when it's time to go home
daughter tells her mother
it's not fair to be the indian everyday

mother agrees

yes, it is not fair
to be the indian everyday

spring creek pow-wow

hands yank back head
a fist full of black hair
as a woman gives another woman the beats
for riding her old man after the 49er

after the woman gets up and mumbles
he wasn't all that thru now puffy lips
a shaky hand flips back feathered brown hair
adjusts ample breasts
and turns on a pointed heel

she fancy dances to a new beat
and crow hops across the flat grass

snaggin blankets

single skins
even not so single skins
carry snaggin blankets
on the pow-wow trail

single skins
even expert and crafty skins
carry snaggin blankets
on the conference circuit

teepee creepin is a cultural exchange
inter-tribals
a sort of inter-treaty negotiation
with a sex clause

unknown reserve

smallpox, tb, processed white sugar
and enriched white flour
english
bad haircuts
and residential school

buffalo wiped from the earth
because it fed and clothed a nation
buffalo bones crushed for fine china

clear-cutting makes way for foreign agriculture
acres and acres of wheat fields
instead of corn, beans and squash
imported white rice versus wild rice
unknown cows replace indigenous buffalo

eagles trapped and killed
for feathers and bald heads
to the point of extinction
they r.i.p. on every green back

this shared history
a legacy
imprinted in my memory

just like paddling the mississauga river
making trails across the plains
to wild rice shores
and blueberry fields
i know my way home

waiting for return of white buffalo

people of the buffalo
live
search
for a new way
waiting
for white buffalo to return

he's the one who sits
on the corner with a card
ask me for the answers
pay what you can

she's the one who used to carry tobacco
in a tight fist
now it falls from a loose grip
she sprinkles the fragrant leaves
down
and sits

they are the ones
waiting

a teen cree girl from manitoba

on november 12, 1971
helen betty osborne
a cree girl from norway house, manitoba
shipped off, fresh from the rez
on the road to higher education
she studies at a high school
with other cree kids
who also feel alone

helen is like other teens of her age
dances, smokes and goes to parties
on friday nights

that night she walks home by herself
a car pulls up to a curb
they all want her to get in and go cruising
but she keeps walking

one gets out of the car
grabs her and shoves her in
the doors slam shut and tires squeal away
black tar strip-marks left on the road

helen betty osborn died in a field
covered in a fresh snowfall

crimson blood sinks
down in mother earth
where this memory lives

life is so complex

sit in smoke-filled bingo halls
offering silent prayers to the bingo god
while dabbing numbers
wishing for niibna zhoonyaa
niimiiwag gamble stomp 24-7-3-6-5

while hungry cubs faint
and inhale solvents
in abandoned school yards
beautiful bannock-stuffed indians
go snagging on friday nights
one fathers thirteen sons and daughters
from just as many women

they all hate him
except one little boy
who loves his daddy
he scribbles *i miss you* with broken crayons
when you coming home?
sealed in a dusty envelope

big brown beautiful bannock-stuffed indians
keep warm around a trash can fire
under a bridge that reeks of urine
listerine bottles circle jagged limbs
winos with fresh breath
sing to the rising flames
licking a night dripping with stars

and here i sit at home
in front of a howard's pawn shop tv
with a blt, bannock, lard and tea
watching re-runs of north of 60
wondering why
this show is so complex

away for a better life

highway 16, the highway of tears
connects prince rupert to prince george
trails from a northern bc home

thumbs hike rides
to a city that calls to young dreamers
promising a better life
and a good time

a car pulls off to the shoulder
wheels crunch over gravel

a quick glance over the shoulder
and a promise to come back to visit

a door opens, closes and echoes into the forest

i crawl into this native land

i.

i dig my fingers deep into moist dark earth
burrow a hole big enough to crawl into
back to where i came from
my mother's womb

ii.

i never asked for a life
in this hell of political shame
where spirits shy away
from this place of predators
vampire hunters gather us
suck our energy
seize our spirit

this native land
vast with natural resources

this sacred earth
no one should go hungry
go without shelter

yet, my brothers, my sisters
are looked upon without compassion
without understanding, hardships and despair
or lives gone wrong

instead, careless hearts
divert eyes so that they never meet
never connect

inside judgment goes on
they deserve to be there on that grimy street
they want to be there on that empty corner
street rats, skids, winos, crack heads
prostitutes and pimps

in this city life
concrete giants hover above tiny bodies
ants trailing behind one by one
in a man-made gridlock
towering prison guards block escape
lined up shoulder to shoulder
along urban routes

manipulated dreams of conquered nations
indians killed during long relay of false truths
words carried on a lifeless breath
unconnected to the mind and heart

treaties signed with alcohol
tools used to trick, seduce and steal
false trades without proper counsel
shared resources for kings and queens

building great civilized and colonized nations
on a land already spoken for
territory with natural laws
people from societies and clans

iii.

my hole is dug deep
i crawl into it
the earth, my mother
stillness in this warm dark womb
wrap arms around knees and hold close to
chest
cradle
the inner thunder that waits

tears are the rain that flows
steady down the mountains
earth shakes and convulses
contractions tremble creation

a full moon rises above
nookomis giiziis medicine
her light cleanses deep inside
and outside of me

hush nadonis
her heart beats lullabies
urging me into dream
my body takes fetal shape

giizis sneaks up in the eastern sky
eyes open, fluttering like a butterfly
stretch stiff limbs on all fours
mukwa crawls out of earth
my mother
brand new

part two

look around us

ocean's wind

on a grassy cliff over the pacific
ocean's wind whispers
a salty breath caresses my bronze skin
i inhale and let it enter these blood traplines

ocean beats into jutting rocks below
heart thumps in my chest and breath comes
arms raise over head, earth to sky
eyes close tight and the countdown begins
spirit lifts and sways in the wind

spring body upward
those seconds in the air are static
until water reaches up
and catches me in her waves
she brings me down
beneath the surface i fall and sink further
suspended as a starfish floating

the air burns in my chest
urging me to release it
spring back to reality
kick my way up

the surface breaks
as i am reaching for a star-crested night
my body floats with the ebb
and swirls in breezy currents
the pacific embraces me whole

hunting

a raven flies
wings with long blue-black feathers
drifting on the wind
currents under body and hovers in the air
raven dives into the creek below
that brims with sockeye

a salmon leaps out of the water
in red and silver arcs
back fins wag and build a momentum
ascending further up stream

bears with pigeon-toed paws
trot over with a swaying heavy head
climb on top of rocks
where the water flows and falls
with mouth open
they bite the springing salmon
canine teeth pierce into the silver belly

eagles swoop
massive wings slow the body down
with talons wide open
preying in the creek
rising with salmon in its golden grip

yet, the salmon move, push and endure
through broken skin and hanging end trails
this gathering place is encoded in memory
bringing salmon home
this long journey
that nothing can stop
not even eagles, ravens or bears

in downtown toronto

delia tracks her copper-toned body
down dundas to an alley off spadina
where a dumpster diver
offers her rice wine and mouldy pizza
the way a priest offers holy eucharist
except this prayer slips between a broken tooth
and a heavy bottom lip

sta-gots! delia shakes her head
maybe some other time i'll break bread with you
and drink your holy blood

delia scans a poster ad: *national aboriginal day*
or was is it *father's recognition day?*
no i think it was *summer solstice feast*
down at the local skins hang-out
but that doesn't really matter to delia
after all, a feast is a *feast*
and free food is *good food*

fry bread, venison and three sister soup guide her
on this vision quest
through the sizzling toronto smog
or a first time sweat at dreamer's rock
only *all my relations* don't work
and the humidity blankets you in sweat
each drops falls and steams on the sidewalk

a sweaty, slightly brown stag
reaches for delia's hand
chh, in her cree-way, *not even*
it's hotter than a bowl of sex
and i am in ass deep in venison already

chhh! ssss! eyyy! all neechees exclaim in unison
and delia goes breasts first into his skinny arms

dusk settles in for a nightcap
while delia and her new/used buck walk away
hands in each other's back pockets
and the door of the sweatlodge
in downtown toronto
swings shut for the night

traffic jam

cars line up at traffic lights
bumper to bumper
faces press against rolled up windows
while fingers make sure doors are locked
praying for a green light
to get the hell out of there

fire ignites from lighters
the red glow of crack pipes
blue smoke exhaled

needles pulled from torn pockets
held in shaky, bony hands
outline of sleeping bodies
in abandoned storefront doorways

the alleyways in between these blocks are
pedestrian-prostitute-addict-dealer-trick-
washroom-delivery-garbage truck
shortcuts for all

broken

brakes: fucked
helmet: cracked
chain: rusty
security: thick chain links and a padlock

ride against traffic exhaust
high on fumes
bumper to ass fucking bumper
ding-ding-ding
screech
horns echo
thud

face plasters into the end of a s-u-f-n-v

between the cracks

right in between the sidewalk cracks
are broken dreams
leaving trails on a concrete path
where threadbare sneakers follow

bend down in jerky movements
pick up bits and pieces of what not
between dirty fingers
scrutinizing
bending back down again
scrutinizing
pebbles and bits of white rock
lick, taste, cast away

as crackheads
go up and down hastings
crows peck between the broken edges
hopping up and down
looking for shiny objects
little chunks of glass and bits of white rock
between busted beaks
ca-ca-cawing

can collectors

an old chinese woman pushes grocery cart
piled high with black bags
bursting with cans and bottles
down to the bottle depot
she joins the line-up on east hastings
can collectors with bags piled high
cruise down vancouver's endtrails
day in
day out
recycling
keeping the streets clean
for some pocket change

walking away from the market

i saw her way past midnight
the air was thick with the sounds of sax
leaking out in sweet soul down streets
bending my ears, swaying my strides
drowning me with swoon
her thoughts
were lightning that danced waltzing blue
and white streaks across the skies

she walks
at night on pond's edge
sings with frogs
echoing in flight

at night
she cradles my dreams
carries tomorrow
and shoos away fear

as rising sun breaks through the lingering mist
morning star sings greeting song
waking from her night walk
in the orbiting sky above

random acts

a little brown girl piles sand high
a castle for a captive princess
a man carrying a briefcase passes by
and remarks that her tepee is cool

with open eyes and open hands

down at the train bridge
that crosses the potomac river
two teen boys trail under a setting red sun
with baskets of the sweetest blueberries
in anishinaabe aking

myiingan holds his nose, squeezes eyes shut
jumps up and out into the welcoming air
his lean body breaks the water, skin slapping
echoes above the tree line

mukwa's eyes follow myiingan's body
shimmering under water
he plunges in
a harpoon after a five-foot-four
sturgeon

sky bleeds into dusk
nokimis giizis peeks over cedars
with a star blanket around her

mukwa's hands linger
over his sun-baked body
unsure of the sweetness of berries
of stars dancing on water, yet… more sure
of eyes meeting on the surface of the unknown

cool currents caress bare skin
wet t-shirts and boxer shorts sink
settles upon mossy rocks
and snagged fishing hooks

mukwa finds myiingan
through the dark moonlit night
with open eyes

one early morning

fire watches, burning for us
as deep sighs escape
and the early dew air sweats blue

twinkling stars fade away
into steam with sun's first touch

water boils in a pot covered in soot
fire crackles to feed it

fire breathes heavy, sending sparks
as deep sighs escape into dew
and the air sweats blue

smoke trails

smoke sneaks
        past night lights
        around dark shades
        through cracks
        under seams

smoke crawls
        across hardwood floors
        up walls painted black

smoke travels
        touches sleeves
        a crumpled pant leg
        a discarded backpack on the scuffed floor

smoke breathes
        nestles in dis-shelved hair
        seeps into sleepy skin

smoke follows
        down a cracked sidewalk to public school
        sits in the back with me in class
        picture of a brown kid at the back
        a smoky cloud hangs around head
        in a grey aura

look around us

the ottawa sun newspaper reads
international day of the elimination of racism
in big black screaming letters

sitting on the blue plush seats
of the new hybrid oc transpo bus
i look around
curious
fearful
sleepy
agitated
regretful
shameful
and angry eyes look away from me

coyotes in the city

i.

coyote sits alone in a coffee shop
at the corner of broadway and commercial
scrutinizing a leather-bound notebook
these days he is fond of writing prose
and the odd naughty limerick

coyote writes about brothers and sisters
who walk down a long dirt road
and never look back

coyote writes about mothers and fathers
who go to the indian bar for drinks
staying way past last call

coyote writes about boys and girls
who learn to dress and cook for themselves
and forge their parents' signatures

coyote writes about grandmas and grandpas
who were taught to write the white man's way
and to speak with no words at all

coyote writes about reservation dogs
who run down city alleys and chase shadows
until their paws bleed

coyote writes about warriors
with broken dreams and stolen hearts
who blockade and have stand-offs
where fires burn with no smoke at all

coyote writes, re-writes and writes again
he wants to be deep and pensive
he writes until he gets a cramp in his hand
and he can't write any more

ii.

coyote prays to nanabush
that she can sing the old songs
on a deer hide hand drum in the kitchen
in front of a stove
in the living room near a window
in the backyard around a small fire

coyote prays to nanabush
that she can dance the old ways
back through sage smoke trails
and to the stars that shift up above

coyote prays to nanabush
that she can tell new stories
with new beginnings
where we don't fall from the sky
or crawl out of the earth
coyote walks across the milky way
where dreams are forever

iii.

coyote sits with many new faces
all of us are there
even some reservation dogs
we all sit with coyote
waiting for him to do something

coyote raises his eyes
to the dancing aurora borealis
he closes his eyes and clears his throat
he taps lightly on his leg
as his song slowly escapes
past his lips, his song is slow
and deliberate like maple sap
after the first frost

he hums it under breath
the song builds inside of him like a fire
it crackles and bursts as coyote begins to sing

and when coyote begins to sing
he gets up, he gets loud
now there's a drum in his hand
and a drum stick in the other
when just moments ago he didn't have either
coyote pounds the drum over and over

he sings songs he never heard before
he sings about how the world was made
out of clay, water, air and definitely fire
he sings about how tough it is
being the only coyote in the city
he sings about reservation dogs
who pretend to be a coyote

he sings about how important faith is
and to be sure that the sun will always rise
he sings about this and about that
until he doesn't know what else to sing about
so he just goes on and on
he beats on the drum till the stick breaks
so he starts banging his head on the drum
over and over again
howling

nanabush steps in
taking the drum away
coyote shrugs his narrow shoulders
and takes a bow

iv.

coyote sits on top of the cn tower and waits
for the words to whisper
for the stories to unravel
for the songs to travel
coyote closes his eyes
and he dreams

v.

park rangers arm themselves with tranquilizers
to take down coyote, to set him free
beyond the urban sprawl
where he can roam free

the problem is that they can't find coyote
and they don't know how clever coyote really is
coyote has always been free

vi.

late one night
while sitting on cracked concrete steps
and exhaling crisp clouds
i hear the sound of clicking nails
tapping along the cluttered streets

one lone coyote in the city
runs and hides behind car wheels
he peeks before darting to the next car
not sure what he is looking for
he sees me from the corner of his eye
and smiles

part three

tending dreams and memories

dreamcatcher

once i had a dream

i lived for a very long time
days, weeks, months and years passed
where i lived in a four-sided home
that had the bare necessities and i was content

until one day i sat in this room
and had an immediate realization
which was weird because this was a dream
i was becoming aware for the first time
like waking up
but in a dream

i realized that something was missing
but i didn't know what
because i've never experienced this before
and as far as i knew this was a new experience
the need and the want consumed me
as i was obsessed with what exactly it was

i slumped against a wall
with a growing tug inside of me
something began to pull me
as this feeling absorbed me
this male figure came into my room
and this room was my entire universe
this is where i lived and was content
until now

i wasn't scared
i knew him
i watched him as he came through the wall
that vanished as he passed through
he asked me the usual questions
as he noticed a drop in my energy
something was definitely not right
yet he left me once again
through that door in the wall
as the door lowered to the floor
i quickly rolled under as it closed

i became a small ball of blue incandescent light
and i flew far from that place
i flew away from a small island
with white sand beaches
that was surrounded by blue green water

i was free and i flew fast out of the stratosphere
into the space beyond
i travelled past other planets
in a swoosh faster than light
i felt the wind in my face
i breathed in freedom

i travelled for a very long time
i was searching
flying past planets and star nations
something deep inside was tugging me
leading me

i came to this planet
and skimmed across the surface
to many places where people dwell
following that tug i came upon this house
i sat on its window's ledge
this is where i was led

inside this dwelling was a family
a woman, a man and two little boys
this was a lively bunch
and this is where i went through that window…

and i opened my eyes

loneliness at two in the morning

a cell vibrates

running dreams:
wolf pack hunts under a moonlit forest

a phone rings

riding dreams:
horseback through tall grass plains

small rocks bounce off a window

swimming dreams:
dolphins in a golden sea of bliss

roll over, rub eyes
various scenarios work their way through

open window?
answer phone?
read text?

in the midst of reaching
and responding to that call
maybe
swimming with dolphins
riding horseback
running with wolves
might just be the cure
for this loneliness at two in the morning

memory lines

from the spout
hot bubbling water rushes between my toes
the tub fills up, embracing my brown belly
nipples lick the surface

flames from tea candles
bounce off ceramic tiles in a line
along the lip of the tub they balance precarious

holding breath as i slip under fragrant salt water
for long moments i lay still
sounds are far away and full of bass

my lungs reach the limit
i fly up and out
waves splash all over the bathroom floor
black smoke rises from doused candles
and stings my eyes

i reach for a plush towel and dry off water drops
there is a book that waits for me
quiet and patient
a would-be lover laying on a bed
wide open, waiting for hands to grab and to hold

word by word
line by line
memory by memory
i taste metaphors and drink similes
until the hot water steams away

wild rice dreams

once i had a dream
flying
i am
the wind

in another dream
i can't get off the ground
and my teeth are flying out of my mouth
as i speak

in another dream
vampires wearing black trench coats
are chasing me
and as they close in
i feel brimstone breath hot on my neck

in another dream
care bears teach me that love conquers all
we hold hands in a circle as we say
we care over and over again
as the vampires turn to smoke
that blows away into nothing

in another dream
i am talking to god
she is beautiful
and when she laughs
she throws back her head
and she tells me to call her nanabush

in another dream
i am a black woman
crossing a bridge
walking hand in hand with my daughter
we are on our way to work
and an old yellow busload of whites goes by
they throw apple cores
overripe tomatoes
and empty pop cans at us
i grip my daughter's hand tighter
and raise my head higher

in another dream
i am washing dishes
and looking out of the window
zaabii runs back and forth
in the back of our métis log house
sasquatch gets closer and closer
until we are face to face
the window is at least
eight feet from the ground
he makes funny faces at me
i wake up laughing
and i smell wild rice, swamp and muskeg

in another dream
i am swimming
and this is the only time
when i really feel free

in another dream
people with no eyes
are taking away my children
i chase after them
as they drive away in a big blue van
but my legs quit working
they turn into iron
and my feet are soldered to the earth

in another dream
i live a different life
from the beginning to the end
when i die i wake up to find out
that i am here now

and at some point i realize and i accept
dreams are like that
reality collides with illusion
or is it all illusion?
or is it real?

breathing deep

insist on breathing deep
moist earth
fresh dew clings
creation

insist on breathing deep
warm summer breeze
pollen flies and lands
collects in my hair
flowering begins at the roots
giveaway for a new life

insist on breathing deep
memories gather in braids
each strand is a story

insist on breathing deep
cedar tree branches fall
gather it in bunches
rub away stress
locked deep within my skin

insist on breathing deep
wind carries songs from east
sun beats into earth
feet pulse on sweet grass
rhythm wakens a spirit song

insist on breathing deep
each and every time

spontaneous love

love as much as you want with whoever you want
love whoever you want as much as you want

it can be innocent like school girls
who skip and sing songs about the boy next door
and give butterfly kisses
in an empty football field

it can be crazy and spontaneous
in the bedroom, kitchen or on the bathroom floor
when heads bump
with every thrust, arch and moan

it can be wild in the middle of a blueberry bush
tangled up in blue so much
you get that faraway look
when fingers trace their way
around purple stains
that remain for days

it can be wild like riding a bucking horse
across wide open plains
together you are one
hips grinding and momentum gathers
as red glowing sun travels
along the mountain ridge with ecstasy

yes, yes, yes, yes… you are
all that
and more

would you?

if i were to tell you a secret
would you be able to keep it?

if i were to tell you
that the universe is vast
and life out there is in here
would you understand?

if i were to tell you
that you are me and i am you
would you accept it?

if i were to tell you
that you should live your life
accept who you are
live without fear and take risks
would you do it?

if i were to tell you
that when you dream
you are really living another life
would you be able to grasp it?

if i were to tell you
that spirits are talking
would you be able to hear?

if i were to tell you
that you are pure spirit and pure love
would you be able to live it?

the 2012 prophecy

there was a mayan who lived in a jungle
along the peak of a mountain
that overlooked the city of teotihuacan
from his perch by a pyramid
as mist cascades around
and images unfold

huge waves curl over the top of the pyramid
over the nearest mountain peak
now a new island

a mountain opens up and spits blood
drips down in globs
rolls along crevices bubbling

earth shudders
rips through grasslands
trenches spread across
devour trees, animals and people
birds spiral counter-clockwise
flying upside down

the mayan blinks his eyes
crawls back down from his perch
goes to the great wall of pictures

in a wooden bowl stained with ochre
he mixes water and powder
with a brush made of fine llama hair

he dips it and draws what he has seen
images haunt him nightly
as he looks at the stars
making marks on a large round tablet
he forms a way of remembering
something more accurate than ever seen before

years later
now called the 2012 prophecy
scientists confirm that it just might be true
the earth's inner world is heating at the core
icebergs melt causing waters to rise
flooding the hudson's bay
creating waves
big enough to surf for the first time ever
the polar bears' skeletons
poke through thick hair as they walk forever
in search of food in a thawed out tundra

the earth shakes and the poles shift slightly
every single time it speeds up
on an axel we spin quicker

throughout human history
life ends
life begins
some ready for change
some deny

and this mayan has another vision
of new people who rise out of the earth

tending memories

imagine:

flying high above
as your body lies
pinned by a man who brings candies
and calls you his favourite niece
on that single-sized bed
with a star blanket
dreams are bridges

memory:

there are some things you forget
and things you remember
like the obsession with counting
how many tiles are on the ceiling
how many stitches are on the quilt
how many seconds are in the dark

fight:

a screen door creeps open
a brown girl in a flower dress
slides against the wall
always keeps her backside safe
she peeks around the corner
then runs at top speed
she tackles him
he flies backwards and lays there

his head oddly-angled
on a cinder-block door step
his blood-shot eyes rolled up
inside his twisted head
candies spilled from a brown bag
on the dry earth
she picks up one of the candies
unwraps it and pops it into her mouth
smiling, she finds the skip in her step
and she never looks back

part four

all in the family

things you used to say

i remember things you used to say
like
i couldn't live
without you

in fact
i couldn't live
with you

and today
i am
living
thriving
without
you

and tomorrow

my heart will beat
stronger
harder
like
never before

because
i know
today
i am
free

letting go

frank's body: found in a fetal shape
carved into the snow and ice
in hand's embrace: an empty listerine bottle
held to parted lips
eyes: salty icicles on lower lashes

later, mom doesn't cry
she kisses his eyes shut
heaves the stiff body to the bathroom
and tries to scrub away many reasons
why her son died before she did

mom clips his finger and toe nails
she rinses his black greying hair in sage
smears on bear grease
braids his hair in sacred sheep's wool
and clothes body in a ribbon shirt
and nylon black slacks

frank's body lies in a open casket
in the living room
uncles, aunts, cousins and friends
shuffle in with food
fried bread, manomin and sandwiches

mom displays frank's belongings
a giveaway, something for everyone
she hands me tattered sneakers
though he never ran, only walked
that long dusty reserve road to town
every day at sunrise
he fetched the daily paper and a bottle of booze

i take the smelly old shoes
leaving mom with family to mourn
i tie the shoe laces
and pitch them in the nearest pine branch
those old kangaroos
dangle against a moonless sky

morning coffee ritual

coffee escapes into steam
it blows from the kitchen to the living room
where it finds me
sitting in my dad's rocker
along a brown shag carpet
i stop to watch, to witness

dad's slippers scrape across the linoleum floor
he stands at the counter
and pours himself a cup of joe
then shuffles back to the kitchen table
sits down on his comfy chair
with an unspoken purpose

in comes my uncle merv
his glasses sit on balding forehead
white curly hair against his brown skin
it reminds me of a lightning across dark sky

uncle merv wears a sky blue fluffy robe
tied loosely at the waist
i imagine many retired steelworkers looking
just as relaxed

good morning, arnold

my dad looks up from his paper
as if he didn't notice him before this moment

good morning, merv

and so it begins

my dad and uncle merv
scoop spoonfuls of sugar into steaming cups
cream splashes into the hot black liquid
it swirls and turns many shades of brown
a mystical spiral together
my dad and uncle merv dip silver-coated spoons
into the coffee

it's a good day, ain't it merv?

uncle merv stares out of the window
nods his head and stirs the spoon

yep... it's a good day

dad stares out of the window too
nods his head while stirring
spoons held expertly
between thick thumbs and nimble fingers
stirring - stirring – stirring
those spoons seem heavy
hitting every single angle in the cup
clinking - clinking - clinking
i had no idea there were so many angles
and somehow that piece of curved metal
finds every single one

yes-siree bob
yes-siree bob
yep it's a good day... yes-siree bob

spoons are cast aside on a shared saucer
dad brings the cup up to his lips
it fogs-up his bi-focals which he ignores
he slurps with eager lips
and uncle merv does the exact same thing
this is nish style surround sound

as i witness this morning ritual
from the next room
i pack up this memory
and let it air out once in a while

granny's fish soup

one time we caught a fish but not just any kind
this fish was a four-foot sturgeon
with a jagged underbite and sharp teeth
its black eyes starting to coat white and stare
with dead eyes fixed on me
until granny seized it by the tail
slapping it on the kitchen table

granny has this gleaming butcher knife
which she used to slice
through its thick silver belly
while she told us fish stories
about all the bigger ones she cleaned before

her belly danced as i watched her hands
stained with fish blood
and fish scales sticking on fingers and arms
even in her granny braids

after fish soup and fry bread filled our bellies
we piled back into the car
a little two-door box on wheels
granny waved from the front steps
still clutching the butcher knife
eager for the next fish
to enter her house

my granny

in the old days
snow drifts were six feet high
walking was a daily activity
and getting up with the sun was a habit

granny offers tea in a mason jar
filled with ice and lemon slices
while mom separates my hair
into three sections and begins to weave

i sit on three big cushions
and wiggle against a yanking comb until
i am left with crooked thick braids that dangle

during the depression era
many grandchildren were left in granny's care
while their mothers and her daughters
worked across the border
in detroit or in soo-michigan factories
sending money home every payday

now granny is a magnificent old lady
her brown-layered skin and bony hands
have bulging veins that my fingertips follow
this road map tells a story
of endurance, stamina and survival

her once brown eyes are now milky blue
that blink back ninety-one years
yet there is a glint of light
that sparkles deep in the iris
between pursed lips she plays the harmonica
roll out the barrel, we'll have a barrel of fun!

granny step dances in the kitchen
that is small, crowded and comfy
relatives are playing
a guitar and a fiddle are picked and strummed
while we all clap, stomp the floor
and cheer granny on

whenever i sit at the kitchen table now
granny's voice whispers
speaking indian stories
to me

fried egg sandwich

granny turns black knob on the stove
it clicks a spark and a blue flame flickers
in the cold morning air

she points to a cupboard behind me
and says with squishy ripe raspberry lips

get the frying pan
the big black one
watch out
it's heavy
it's iron

she reaches into waiting refrigerator
in one hand a stick of butter
an oval brown egg in the other

she passes butter knife to me
i slice off a chunk from the yellow hard brick
it sizzles and beads dancing
along a slick black rink

she passes me cold egg
in my head i picture a buoy
oddly bouncing in water
as i feel this uneven weight in my hand

i crack the egg along the thickness of the rim
it breaks open into a rigid crevice
halfway across
spilling gooey, white slippery liquid
as it drips down the side
it sticks and turns white

i grab granny's wooden spatula
it has a groove in it
a grip - a hand's home
i poke to pierce a hole
into the yellow bulging eye
it erupts like a volcano's hot golden lava
that spills over the edge
i sprinkle salt
it crystallizes and sticks to the surface
i sprinkle pepper
black specks on gold

i let the egg crisp brown around the edges
then slip the wooden spatula under its body
and flip the egg over
it sizzles and pops

i smile big and wide
quick with pride
grandma smiles too
exposing a pink slick gum line

the smell of burning bread fills the air
under the heat of electric wires
toast pops up and flies up into the air
and lands on a bone china plate
granny's wrinkly hands are quick
she is an anishinaabe ninja

she scrapes off some butter
the knife glides easily over the rough terrain
the yellow disappears
sinking deep into crusty pockets
tiny puddles of salty goodness

i rescue the egg from the heat that lingers
lay it on one of the glistening pieces of toast
then put the other slice down on top
because it yearns to be a part of it all
i cut it in half, diagonally from corner to corner
and offer the fried egg sandwich to granny

her gums sink in
she tears through the toast and the egg
then sets the remains on the plate
with no distinct teeth markings
just jagged edges

her face shrinks into itself with every bite
over and over again
her eyes are black, glossy and bright

mmmm… mmmm
just like mine

how granny braids

we sit at granny's kitchen table
and sip red rose tea
a true indian drink
and tear apart day-old bannock
we dip it into a tub of lard
these are hard times
so they tell us on that transistor radio
but we just like the taste
left on our tongues
it makes our words slippery

granny props me up on pillows
pulls on my hair
runs her fingers through knots
and begins to braid

granny tells stories as she braids
they, she says, are my memory
we braid our hair to remember
and to honour our ancestors
it's us, three sisters, three strands of hair
we become whole
me, you and them

granny settles her agile body
on a stool by the kitchen table
she taps her wrinkly fingers to some old ditty
my tiny fingers wrap around her baby finger
and i make a wish to remember
how granny braids

when i was a child

the grass grows a deeper shade of green
behind granny's empty shed
where an outhouse used to stand
now all that remains are broken down walls

as kids we would carry flashlights
in our chubby hands
in the middle of the night
one after another
pushing and screaming
running to that putrid place

sometimes one of us would wait outside
shining the light into the darkness
even though granny told us not to
because of the spirits laying in the shadows
and we might see something
that wasn't meant for our eyes
but we still flashed the light

i was eight at the time
shaking the light into the forest night
i was listening so hard
that i heard the beat of my heart
blood pumping into my brain
the crunch of leaves under my small feet
the crack of branches
somewhere in the distance
i would turn the light one way
then the other way

eyes shining, reflecting in the shadows
blinking green eyes catch my attention
my feet become part of the moss
beneath, growing tentacles holding me tight
restricting the scream caught in my throat
like fish in a net struggling for freedom

the door crashes behind me
which loosens that scream
and it echoes into the night
i run followed by my cousin
our shadows chasing to catch up to us
as granny opens the door, we fly into the house
our breaths come in rasps
and that familiar *ee-yaa* from granny

there is a scratching at the screen door
my cousin and i look at each other
we stand behind granny and peak around her

granny peaks through the curtains
then opens the door a tiny bit
in comes a little moochie and she sniffs my legs
licking at the scrapes
from low blueberry branches
she whimpers blinking up at me

all this fades away as i walk towards
that deeper shade of green
and those brief moments of not knowing
whose glowing eyes those were
and how our imagination played us

all in the family

passive aggressive:
love you: hate you
come here: go away
go ahead: don't you dare
take your time: hurry up
no, no it's okay: what the hell?

obsessive compulsive disorder:
take three drinks
wipe mouth on napkin, re-fold
take three drinks
wipe mouth on napkin, re-fold

put spoon next to saucer
at ninety degree angle

get up check the door
open it, look down hallway
close the door, turn the lock
peak through pigeon hole

do it again
and again
and again

days are long
eighty six thousand four hundred seconds
in one day
i counted

schizophrenia:

watch out
camera points
targets
focuses
on every movement

it's hidden
in these plastered walls
see those eyes?
in that picture
there
they follow

don't eat that food
it's poisoned
inedible
it's killing me
slowly

my spirit
scratches
into earth
burrow to safety

multiple personalities:

why is peter taking the long way?
stay out of it mary
why? do i have to?
don't tell mary what to do, jesus!
me?
yeah you

peter walks down the street
hands flop around
from arms going every which way
head bending in conversation
back and forth, call and answer

now look what you've done
don't blame me, mary
jesus, i'm not blaming you
i think it's both your fault
right peter?
peter?
whose peter?

peter rubs temples
bangs head against high brick wall
shut up
shut up
shut up

the final frontier

did you know that we are floating in space?
my daughter asks me

i ponder this question
let it blow my mind
as it branches off into many splinters
let it sink deep into my skin
deep into my bones
deep into…

well… mother?

she pauses for a long deep sigh
the kind only a teenager could do
rolling her eyes up and away
perfecting her new muscle
like she is learning how to tie her shoes
then she begins more sincere and direct

the earth is a star in the milky way
we live on a planet, a big blue planet
which is almost seventy-five percent water
and we're floating around in space!

i am listening and still trying to grasp
earth being in space, the immensity of it all
i don't think i ever thought about it
this way before
seriously…

seriously?
she says this like she just read my mind
then bursts out laughing
and then just like a bunch of kids
she jumps all over it

mom… do you mean
that you never thought about this before?
she continues with more hysterical laughter

really, i don't think i have, not like this

the hysterical laughter stops rather abruptly
like she didn't want to hit a bump at full speed
she stops momentarily, gathering all her wits
all the angles she can come from
a mathematician, yes, she is calculating
before she has a chance to open her mouth

i say, *that is so cool, man*
when you really think about it that way
because you know, i never thought
about the earth being a planet
and like we're floating around in space
and space, man… is like so big
like that just blows my freaking mind, man

my daughter walks away laughing
i call out to her
floating around in space, eh?
so does it mean we're aliens?

hockey night in canada

last night the queen dropped the puck
at the gm place
where the right price gets you a nosebleed seat
while you scrounge for a parking space
along the border of the downtown eastside

last night the queen dropped the puck
at the centre ice
taking pointers from her escorts
hockey coaches, captains, goalies
and even me who favours no team

last night the queen dropped the puck
right in front of
beer-guzzling
peanut-popping
popcorn-chucking
pot-bellied
and war-painted faces

as the queen drop the puck
dragon chasers nod
under a star-crested night
in andy livingston park
a tribe treks back to the georgia viaduct
cut-out cardboard condos
a brother is holed up in a corner
trying real hard not to think about the next fix

acknowledgements

Chi-miigwetch for the blood and memory that flows through me like lava.

Chi-miigwetch to my mother, Barbara, who has always supported me. And Chi-Miigwetch to my father, Arnold, who always loved me from afar. Thank you to my brothers Fred, JR, and Kevin. Thank you to my sisters Kristin, Michelle, Patty, Leena, Kelly, Samantha, Tracey, and Ruby. Thank you to my nieces Cheyenne, Jessica, and Jayd, to my nephews Jake and Koulton. Thank you to all my cousins, my aunties, and my uncles for being constant. And thank you to all my friends, who have always stood behind me and held me up.

Thank you to all the writers and teachers who have inspired me: Dennis Saddleman, Larry Nicholson, Beverly Hungry-Wolf, Sherman Alexie, Eden Robinson, Joseph Dandurand, David Groulx, Eion Colfer, John Irving, Toni Morrison, Marilyn Dumont, Kateri Akiwenzie-Damm, Sharron Proulx-Turner, Linda Rogers, Carl Sagan, and Kelley Armstrong. Your words have filled me with inspiration and encouraged me to forge on.

Chi-miigwetch to the grandfathers, grandmothers, and our ancestors, who watch over us with spirit eyes, guide us, and give us strength. And a very special thank you to our elders and our spiritual leaders, who carry the old ways and who are always there to give us hope.

I would also like to extend my sincere thanks to the Indigenous Arts Program at the Banff Centre for the Arts and the Canada Council for the Arts for bringing me back to a place I call home. Thank you to my mentors, Beverly, Marilyn, Kateri, Witi, Lee, Crystal, Kathy, Chris, and Sandra, for their vision and dedication. Thank you to Richard Van Camp for his support and very insightful review of the book.

Chi-Miigwetch to Marilyn Dumont for helping me with this poetry collection and giving me such a great feedback. Chi-miigwetch to Larry, Gord, Chandra, Patty, Joseph, Samee, and Linda for offering comments on the final draft.

I would like to acknowledge the financial support of the Ontario Arts Council. Thank you very much.